Iceland: The Land of Fire and Ice

A Winter Wonderland of Northern Lights, Geysers, and Glaciers: An Insider's Guide to Exploring Iceland's Hidden Treasures

David S. Porter

D1712820

Table of Contents

Introduction

Iceland: The Land of Fire and Ice

I've always been drawn to the idea of Iceland. The stark contrast between its fiery volcanic landscapes and its icy glaciers has captivated my imagination for as long as I can remember. It's a place where the raw power of nature is on full display, where ancient myths and legends intertwine with modern reality.

My journey to Iceland began on a crisp winter morning. As the plane descended, I was greeted by a breathtaking vista of snow-capped mountains, vast glaciers, and icy fjords. The landscape was so alien yet strangely familiar, as if I had stepped into a painting or a dream.

Stepping off the plane, I was immediately struck by the biting cold. The air was crisp and clean, carrying with it a hint of sulfur and the salty tang of the sea. As we drove from the airport, I was captivated by the ever-changing scenery. One moment, we were passing through a desolate volcanic desert, the next, we were winding our way through a lush green valley.

One of my first stops was the Golden Circle, a popular tourist route that takes in some of Iceland's most iconic sights. Our first stop was Thingvellir National Park, a UNESCO World Heritage Site where the Eurasian and North American tectonic plates are slowly drifting apart. The park is a geological marvel, with towering cliffs, crystal-clear lakes, and a network of lava fields.

From Thingvellir, we headed to Geysir, a geothermal area famous for its hot springs and geysers. The most famous geyser is Strokkur, which erupts every few minutes, sending a towering plume of hot water and steam into the sky. It was a truly awe-inspiring sight, and I couldn't help but feel a sense of wonder and respect for the power of nature.

Our final stop on the Golden Circle was Gullfoss, one of the most beautiful waterfalls in Iceland. The waterfall plunges into a deep canyon, creating a deafening roar that echoes through the valley. The water is a stunning turquoise color, and the surrounding landscape is a mix of snow-capped mountains and lush green meadows.

After our tour of the Golden Circle, we headed to the South Coast, a region known for its dramatic landscapes and stunning waterfalls. Our first stop was Seljalandsfoss, a waterfall that cascades down a cliff face and disappears behind a curtain of rock. It's possible to walk behind the waterfall, offering a unique perspective on this natural wonder.

Our next stop was Skógafoss, another impressive waterfall that plunges down a cliff face into a deep pool. The waterfall is surrounded by lush green meadows and offers stunning views of the surrounding mountains and glaciers.

From Skógafoss, we continued our journey along the South Coast, stopping at Reynisfjara Black Sand Beach. The beach is famous for its black sand, towering sea cliffs, and distinctive rock formations. It's also a popular spot for birdwatching, with a variety of seabirds nesting in the cliffs.

As we continued our journey, we were treated to a stunning display of the Northern Lights. The sky was filled with swirling bands of green, pink, and purple light, dancing across the heavens. It was a magical experience that I will never forget.

Iceland is a truly unique and unforgettable destination. Its stunning landscapes, fascinating culture, and friendly people make it a must-visit for anyone seeking a truly extraordinary travel experience.

A Winter Wonderland

The plane descended through a blanket of fluffy clouds, revealing a landscape transformed into a winter wonderland. Snow-capped mountains stretched as far as the eye could see, their peaks kissed by the soft glow of the setting sun. Below, a patchwork of frozen lakes and rivers shimmered in the fading light.

As we touched down, a gust of icy wind whipped through the open door of the terminal. The air was crisp and invigorating, carrying with it the scent of pine and snow. Bundling up in my warmest layers, I stepped out into the winter wonderland.

The town was a picture-perfect scene. Snow-covered cottages lined the streets, their windows glowing warmly. The town square was a bustling hub of activity, with locals and tourists alike enjoying the winter festivities. A towering Christmas tree stood proudly in the center, its branches adorned with twinkling lights and colorful ornaments.

I wandered through the snow-covered streets, taking in the sights and sounds. Children played in the snow, building snowmen and having snowball fights. A horse-drawn sleigh clattered along the cobbled streets, its bells jingling merrily.

As night fell, the town was transformed into a magical winter wonderland. The streets were illuminated by strings of fairy lights, casting a warm glow on the snow-covered buildings. The sky above was a canvas of stars, their light reflecting in the icy surface of the frozen lake.

I decided to take a winter walk through the nearby forest. The trees were heavy with snow, their branches bent under the weight. The forest was eerily quiet, broken only by the occasional crunch of snow beneath my feet. A sense of peace and tranquility washed over me as I wandered through the winter wonderland.

Suddenly, I heard a rustling sound. A small herd of deer emerged from the trees, their breath misting in the cold air. They stood watching me for a moment, their large, gentle eyes filled with curiosity. Then, they turned and disappeared back into the forest.

As I made my way back to town, I couldn't help but feel a sense of awe and wonder. This winter wonderland was a truly magical place, a place where time seemed to stand still. I knew that I would never forget this experience.

Why Visit Iceland in Winter

Iceland in winter is a truly magical place. The landscape is transformed into a winter wonderland, with snow-capped mountains, frozen waterfalls, and shimmering glaciers. But there's so much more to Iceland in winter than just its stunning scenery.

One of the biggest draws of visiting Iceland in winter is the chance to see the Northern Lights. This breathtaking natural phenomenon is caused by the interaction of charged particles from the sun with the Earth's atmosphere. The result is a dazzling display of colorful lights that dance across the sky.

I was lucky enough to witness the Northern Lights during my trip to Iceland. We drove out of the city and found a secluded spot away from the light pollution. As the sky darkened, the Northern Lights began to appear. They were a mesmerizing sight, with swirling bands of green, pink, and purple light. It was an experience that I will never forget.

Another reason to visit Iceland in winter is the opportunity to participate in winter sports. Iceland offers a variety of winter activities, including skiing, snowboarding, snowmobiling, and ice skating. There are several ski resorts in Iceland, with slopes suitable for all levels of skiers and snowboarders.

I spent a day skiing at the Hlíðarfjall ski resort near Akureyri. The slopes were well-maintained, and the scenery was breathtaking. As I skied down the mountain, I was surrounded by snow-capped peaks and a crystal-clear blue sky. It was a truly exhilarating experience.

Iceland in winter is also a great place to experience Icelandic culture. The Icelandic people are incredibly friendly and welcoming. They are proud of their heritage and traditions, and they are happy to share them with visitors.

I had the opportunity to attend a traditional Icelandic Christmas celebration. The event was held in a cozy farmhouse, and it was filled with music, food, and laughter. We enjoyed a delicious feast of Icelandic delicacies, including smoked lamb, pickled fish, and rye bread. It was a wonderful way to experience Icelandic culture firsthand.

Finally, visiting Iceland in winter is simply a beautiful experience. The landscape is transformed into a winter wonderland, and the air is crisp and clean. It's a place where you can truly relax and appreciate the beauty of nature.

If you're looking for a unique and unforgettable travel experience, I highly recommend visiting Iceland in winter. It's a place that will leave you with memories that will last a lifetime.

Planning Your Trip

When to Visit Iceland: A Burst of Winter Magic

Iceland is a captivating country that offers a unique blend of natural wonders and cultural experiences. While it can be visited year-round, winter presents a particularly magical time to explore this Nordic gem. Here's a burst of reasons why:

The Northern Lights: One of the most compelling reasons to visit Iceland in winter is to witness the mesmerizing Aurora Borealis. These dancing lights paint the night sky with vibrant hues, creating an unforgettable spectacle. The best time to see the Northern Lights is from September to April, when the nights are long and dark.

A Winter Wonderland: Iceland transforms into a breathtaking winter wonderland, with snow-covered landscapes, frozen waterfalls, and glistening glaciers. The stark beauty of the Icelandic winter is truly awe-inspiring. From December to February, you'll experience the peak of winter, with the shortest days and the coldest temperatures.

Fewer Crowds: While Iceland attracts a steady stream of visitors throughout the year, winter offers a more peaceful experience. With fewer crowds, you can enjoy the country's attractions without the hustle and bustle. This is especially true for popular destinations like the Blue Lagoon and the Golden Circle.

Unique Winter Activities: Winter in Iceland presents a range of unique activities that are unavailable during other seasons. Snowmobiling on glaciers, ice caving, dog sledding, and skiing are just a few of the thrilling experiences you can enjoy.

Festive Atmosphere: The winter months in Iceland are filled with a festive atmosphere. Christmas markets, cozy cafes, and charming villages create a magical ambiance. You can experience traditional Icelandic customs and enjoy delicious local cuisine.

Getting to Iceland:

There are several ways to reach Iceland:

- By Air: Keflavík International Airport is the main gateway to Iceland. Numerous airlines offer direct flights from major cities around the world.
- By Sea: While less common, it's possible to reach Iceland by cruise ship. Several cruise lines offer itineraries that include Iceland as a destination.

Choosing the Right Airport:

Keflavík International Airport is located approximately 50 kilometers (31 miles) from Reykjavík, the capital city. It's the most convenient option for most travelers. However, if you're flying from a smaller city or prefer a more regional airport, you may have limited flight options.

Considering Alternative Airports:

In addition to Keflavík International Airport, there are a few smaller airports in Iceland, including Akureyri Airport in the north and Reykjavík Airport in the capital city. These airports may offer more direct flights from certain regions, but they often have fewer flight options and higher fares.

Transportation in Iceland: Navigating the Icelandic Roads

Iceland offers a variety of transportation options to suit different preferences and budgets. Here's a burst of information to help you navigate the Icelandic roads:

Car Rental: Renting a car is a popular choice for exploring Iceland. It offers flexibility and allows you to reach remote areas that may not be accessible by public transportation. However, driving in Iceland requires caution due to challenging road conditions, especially in winter.

Public Transportation: Iceland has a well-developed public transportation system, including buses and ferries. Buses connect major cities and towns, while ferries provide transportation to remote areas. However, public transportation may be limited in certain regions, especially during off-peak seasons.

Self-Drive Tours: Organized self-drive tours offer a convenient way to explore Iceland. These tours include car rental, accommodation, and pre-planned itineraries. They are a great option for those who want a hassle-free experience.

Accommodation in Iceland: A Cozy Retreat

Iceland offers a range of accommodation options to suit different budgets and preferences. Here's a burst of ideas for your stay:

Hotels and Guesthouses: Hotels and guesthouses are widely available throughout Iceland, offering a range of amenities and services. From budget-friendly options to luxury accommodations, you can find a suitable place to stay in most towns and cities.

Vacation Rentals: Renting a vacation home or apartment can be a great way to experience Icelandic culture and enjoy more privacy. Many vacation rentals are located in scenic areas, offering stunning views and a peaceful atmosphere.

Camping: For a more adventurous and budget-friendly experience, camping is a popular option in Iceland. There are numerous campsites available throughout the country, offering basic facilities and stunning natural surroundings.

Farm Stays: Farm stays provide a unique opportunity to experience Icelandic rural life. You can stay on a working farm, participate in farm activities, and enjoy delicious homemade food.

Unique Accommodations: Iceland offers a variety of unique accommodation options, such as ice hotels, igloos, and geothermal hot springs. These options provide a truly unforgettable experience.

Choosing the Right Accommodation:

When selecting accommodation in Iceland, consider the following factors:

- Location: Decide whether you want to stay in a central location or in a more remote area.
- Budget: Determine your budget and choose accommodation that fits your financial constraints.
- Amenities: Consider the amenities that are important to you, such as Wi-Fi, parking, and breakfast.
- Experience: Decide whether you prefer a traditional hotel experience or a more unique accommodation option.

Budget Planning: A Financial Adventure in Iceland

Iceland, while not the most budget-friendly destination, offers a range of options to suit different travel styles and budgets. Here's a burst of tips to help you plan your finances:

Accommodation:

- Hostels: Hostels are a great way to save money on accommodation. They offer shared rooms and basic amenities, but they can be a good option for budget travelers.
- Camping: Camping is another affordable option, especially during the summer months. There are numerous campsites available throughout Iceland, offering basic facilities and stunning natural surroundings.
- Farm Stays: Farm stays are a unique and budget-friendly option. They offer basic accommodations and delicious homemade food.

Transportation:

- Public Transportation: Buses and ferries are relatively affordable options for getting around Iceland.
- Hitchhiking: Hitchhiking is a popular way to travel in Iceland, especially during the summer months. It's a great way to meet locals and save money on transportation.
- Self-Drive Tours: Organized self-drive tours can be a cost-effective option, especially if you're traveling with a group. They often include car rental, accommodation, and pre-planned itineraries.

Food:

- Grocery Stores: Shopping at grocery stores is a great way to save money on food. You can prepare your own meals and snacks, which can be significantly cheaper than eating out.
- Local Markets: Visit local markets to find fresh, affordable produce and local delicacies.

- Food Banks: If you're on a very tight budget, consider visiting a food bank. These organizations provide food to people in need.

Activities:
- Free Activities: There are many free activities to enjoy in Iceland, such as hiking, exploring national parks, and visiting museums.
- Group Tours: Joining group tours can be a cost-effective way to experience Iceland's attractions.
- Off-Peak Season: Traveling during the off-peak season can help you save money on activities and accommodations.

Packing List: Essentials for Your Icelandic Adventure

Packing for Iceland requires careful consideration due to the unpredictable weather and varied terrain. Here's a burst of essential items to pack:

Clothing:

- Warm layers: Base layers, fleece jackets, and waterproof outerwear are essential for staying warm.
- Waterproof boots: Good quality waterproof boots are a must-have for exploring Iceland's rugged terrain.
- Hats and gloves: Keep your head and hands warm with hats and gloves.
- Sunglasses: Protect your eyes from the sun, even on cloudy days.

Equipment:

- Backpack: A comfortable backpack is essential for carrying your belongings.
- Camera: Capture the stunning landscapes of Iceland with a good camera.
- Tripod: A tripod is helpful for taking photos in low light conditions.
- First-aid kit: Pack a first-aid kit to treat minor injuries.

Other Essentials:

- Travel documents: Passport, visa (if required), and travel insurance.
- Cash and credit cards: Bring a mix of cash and credit cards for your expenses.
- International adapter: If you're using electronic devices, bring an international adapter.
- Reusable water bottle: Stay hydrated by bringing a reusable water bottle.
- Snacks: Pack snacks to keep you going between meals.

Must-See Attractions

Golden Circle:

Thingvellir National Park: A Geological Marvel

Thingvellir National Park, a UNESCO World Heritage Site, is one of the most iconic destinations in Iceland. Located in the Golden Circle, a popular tourist route, it offers a unique blend of geological wonders, historical significance, and breathtaking natural beauty.

A Geological Wonderland:

Thingvellir is a geological marvel where the Eurasian and North American tectonic plates are slowly drifting apart. This tectonic activity has created a dramatic landscape of fissures, faults, and volcanic fields. The most striking feature is the Almannagjá rift, a deep fissure that stretches for several kilometers. Walking along the rift, you can feel the raw power of the Earth as the plates move apart.

Historical Significance:

Thingvellir is not only a geological wonder but also a place of great historical importance. In 930 AD, Iceland's first parliament, the Alþingi, was established here. The Alþingi was one of the oldest functioning parliaments in the world and played a crucial role in shaping Iceland's history.

Þingvellir Lake:

Þingvellir Lake, the largest natural lake in Iceland, is located within the national park. The lake is surrounded by stunning scenery, including towering cliffs, lush meadows, and volcanic craters. You can enjoy swimming, boating, and fishing in the lake, or simply relax and admire the breathtaking views.

Silfra Fissure:

One of the most popular activities in Thingvellir is snorkeling or diving in the Silfra Fissure. This fissure is filled with crystal-clear water that has been filtered through volcanic rock for centuries. The visibility in Silfra is exceptional, allowing you to see the underwater landscape in stunning detail.

Hiking Trails:

Thingvellir National Park offers a variety of hiking trails to suit different fitness levels and interests. You can hike through the rift valley, explore the surrounding forests, or climb to the top of a nearby hill for panoramic views.

Tips for Visiting Thingvellir:

- Dress Warmly: Iceland's weather can be unpredictable, especially in winter. Dress in warm layers and wear waterproof clothing.

- Bring Good Hiking Shoes: The terrain in Thingvellir can be uneven, so it's important to wear comfortable hiking shoes.
- Plan Your Visit: Thingvellir is a popular destination, so it's a good idea to plan your visit in advance. Consider visiting during the off-peak season to avoid crowds.
- Respect the Environment: Thingvellir is a fragile ecosystem. Please respect the environment by staying on designated trails and avoiding disturbing wildlife.

Thingvellir National Park is a must-visit destination for anyone traveling to Iceland. Its unique combination of geological wonders, historical significance, and natural beauty makes it a truly unforgettable experience.

Geysir Geothermal Area: A Boiling Hot Experience

Geysir Geothermal Area, located in the Golden Circle, is a must-see destination in Iceland. This geothermal field is home to numerous hot springs, mud pots, and geysers, offering a fascinating glimpse into the Earth's inner workings.

The Great Geysir:

The area's namesake, the Great Geysir, was once one of the most powerful geysers in the world. However, its eruptions have become less frequent in recent years due to seismic activity. Despite its reduced activity, the Great Geysir remains a captivating sight, with its towering cone and steaming pool.

Strokkur Geyser:

While the Great Geysir may be less active, its neighbor, Strokkur, is a reliable performer. Strokkur erupts every few minutes, sending a plume of hot water and steam soaring into the sky. The eruptions are unpredictable, adding to the excitement and anticipation.

Other Geothermal Features:

In addition to the geysers, the Geysir Geothermal Area is home to a variety of other geothermal features. You can explore bubbling mud pots, steaming fumaroles, and colorful mineral deposits. The area's unique landscape is a testament to the powerful forces at work beneath the Earth's surface.

Tips for Visiting Geysir Geothermal Area:

- Dress Warmly: The area can be windy and cold, especially in winter. Dress in warm layers and wear waterproof clothing.

- Stay on Designated Paths: For your safety and to protect the delicate geothermal features, stay on the designated paths.
- Be Cautious: Some areas of the geothermal field are hot and can be dangerous. Exercise caution and follow the posted warnings.
- Take Photos: The Geysir Geothermal Area offers stunning photo opportunities. Capture the beauty of the geysers, mud pots, and surrounding landscape.

Visiting the Geysir Geothermal Area is a unique and unforgettable experience. Witnessing the power of nature firsthand is a truly awe-inspiring sight.

Gullfoss Waterfall: A Majestic Cascade

Gullfoss Waterfall, another highlight of the Golden Circle, is one of the most iconic waterfalls in Iceland. Its powerful cascade and stunning beauty have made it a popular destination for visitors from around the world.

A Double Cascade:

Gullfoss is a double waterfall, consisting of two tiers that plunge into a deep canyon. The upper tier drops 11 meters (36 feet), followed by a second drop of 21 meters (69 feet). The waterfall's name, which means "golden falls," is derived from the golden hue that the water often takes on when the sun shines on it.

A Natural Wonder:

Gullfoss is a truly breathtaking sight. The powerful flow of water creates a deafening roar that echoes through the canyon. The surrounding landscape is also impressive, with towering cliffs and lush green meadows.

A Sustainable Future:

In the early 20th century, there were plans to build a hydroelectric power plant at Gullfoss. However, local environmentalists fought to protect the waterfall, and their efforts were ultimately successful. Today, Gullfoss is a protected area, ensuring its preservation for future generations.

Tips for Visiting Gullfoss:

- Dress Warmly: The area around Gullfoss can be windy and cold, especially in winter. Dress in warm layers and wear waterproof clothing.
- Take a Walk: There are several walking paths around Gullfoss, offering different viewpoints of the waterfall.
- Avoid the Crowds: Gullfoss is a popular destination, so try to visit during the off-peak season to avoid crowds.
- Respect the Environment: Gullfoss is a fragile ecosystem. Please respect the environment by staying on designated paths and avoiding disturbing wildlife.

South Coast:

The South Coast of Iceland is home to two of the most breathtaking waterfalls in the country: Seljalandsfoss and Skógafoss. These waterfalls are both known for their unique beauty and charm, and they are a must-see for any visitor to Iceland.

Seljalandsfoss:

Seljalandsfoss is a 60-meter-tall waterfall that is located just off the Ring Road. The waterfall is unique in that it is possible to walk behind it, making it a popular spot for photographers. The path behind the waterfall is narrow and can be slippery, so it is important to be careful when walking.

The waterfall is also surrounded by beautiful scenery, including lush green meadows and rolling hills. There are several viewpoints where you can enjoy the view of the waterfall, including a path that leads to the top of the cliff.

Skógafoss:

Skógafoss is another 60-meter-tall waterfall that is located on the South Coast of Iceland. It is one of the most powerful waterfalls in the country, and its water can be seen from miles away.

Skógafoss is also unique in that it is possible to climb to the top of the waterfall. There are 527 steps that lead to the top, and the view from there is breathtaking. The waterfall is also surrounded by beautiful scenery, including lush green meadows, forests, and mountains.

Visiting Seljalandsfoss and Skógafoss:

Seljalandsfoss and Skógafoss are both located on the Ring Road, so they are easily accessible by car. The waterfalls are also about 15 minutes apart by car, so it is possible to visit both in one day.

There are several parking lots near both waterfalls, and there are also public restrooms and picnic areas available.

Visiting Seljalandsfoss and Skógafoss is a truly unforgettable experience. These waterfalls are two of the most beautiful and majestic natural wonders in Iceland.

Reynisfjara Black Sand Beach: A Dark Beauty

Reynisfjara Black Sand Beach is a striking and unique destination on the South Coast of Iceland. Its dark, volcanic sand creates a stark contrast against the crashing waves and towering sea cliffs. This beach is a must-visit for those seeking a dramatic and otherworldly landscape.

The Black Sand:

The black sand at Reynisfjara is formed from volcanic ash that has been eroded by the ocean. The sand is fine-grained and has a velvety texture. It's a popular spot for sunbathing and taking photos, but be cautious of the strong currents and unpredictable waves.

The Sea Cliffs:

Reynisdrangar, a pair of sea stacks that rise from the ocean, are a prominent feature of Reynisfjara. These basalt columns are said to be trolls that were turned to stone by sunlight. The cliffs are also home to a variety of seabirds, including puffins and guillemots.

The Cave:

Reynisfjara is also home to a sea cave that can be explored at low tide. The cave is a popular spot for photography and offers a unique perspective of the beach and the surrounding cliffs.

Tips for Visiting Reynisfjara:

- Check the Tides: The sea cave is only accessible at low tide. Check the tide times before you visit.
- Dress Warmly: The weather on the South Coast can be unpredictable, even in summer. Dress in warm layers and waterproof clothing.
- Be Cautious of the Waves: The waves at Reynisfjara can be very strong. Do not swim or wade into the water.
- Respect the Environment: The beach is a fragile ecosystem. Please respect the environment by leaving no trace.

Vatnajökull National Park: A Land of Ice and Fire

Vatnajökull National Park is the largest national park in Europe and encompasses a vast area of glaciers, volcanoes, and other natural wonders. It's a must-visit destination for anyone interested in exploring the raw beauty of Iceland.

Vatnajökull Glacier:

The park's namesake, Vatnajökull, is the largest glacier in Europe. The glacier covers an area of approximately 8,400 square kilometers (3,240 square miles) and is home to several ice caves. Visitors can take guided tours of the ice caves, which offer a unique and unforgettable experience.

Volcanoes and Hot Springs:

Vatnajökull National Park is also home to several active volcanoes, including Öræfajökull and Grímsvötn. These volcanoes have shaped the landscape of the park and have caused significant eruptions in the past. The park is also home to numerous hot springs, including the famous Blue Lagoon.

Hiking and Wildlife:

There are many hiking trails in Vatnajökull National Park, offering opportunities to explore the diverse landscapes of the park. Visitors can also spot a variety of wildlife, including Arctic foxes, reindeer, and birds.

Tips for Visiting Vatnajökull National Park:

- Plan Your Visit: Vatnajökull National Park is a large area, so it's important to plan your visit in advance. Decide which areas you want to visit and how much time you have to spend there.
- Dress Warmly: The weather in Vatnajökull can be unpredictable, even in summer. Dress in warm layers and waterproof clothing.
- Bring Good Hiking Shoes: There are many hiking trails in the park, so it's important to wear comfortable hiking shoes.
- Respect the Environment: Vatnajökull National Park is a fragile ecosystem. Please respect the environment by staying on designated trails and avoiding disturbing wildlife.

Northern Lights:

Chasing the Aurora Borealis: A Guide to Northern Lights Viewing in Iceland

Iceland is a prime destination for observing the Northern Lights, also known as the Aurora Borealis. These mesmerizing celestial displays are caused by collisions between charged particles from the sun and the Earth's atmosphere. Here's a guide to help you maximize your chances of witnessing this natural phenomenon:

Best Viewing Spots:

- Remote Locations: To avoid light pollution, head to areas away from cities and towns. The further north you go, the better your chances of seeing the Northern Lights.
- Northern Iceland: Akureyri and its surrounding areas are popular spots for Aurora hunting due to their high latitude and relatively low light pollution.

- Snæfellsnes Peninsula: This peninsula offers stunning landscapes and opportunities for Aurora viewing, especially during the off-season.
- Vatnajökull National Park: The vast expanse of Vatnajökull glacier provides a dramatic backdrop for Aurora displays.
- Thingvellir National Park: This UNESCO World Heritage Site offers beautiful scenery and opportunities for Aurora viewing.

Tips for Aurora Hunting:
- Check the Aurora Forecast: Several online resources provide real-time Aurora forecasts. Keep an eye on these forecasts to determine the best time for viewing.
- Dress Warmly: Even in summer, temperatures can drop significantly at night. Dress in warm layers and wear waterproof clothing.
- Be Patient: Aurora displays can be unpredictable. Be patient and enjoy the experience, even if you don't see the lights immediately.

- Find a Dark Spot: Look for a location away from artificial light sources. The darker the sky, the better your chances of seeing the Aurora.
- Look Up: The Aurora typically appears as a faint glow on the horizon. Look up towards the sky to catch the display.
- Avoid Light Pollution: Turn off all lights and avoid using flash photography to preserve your night vision.
- Stay Up Late: The Aurora is most likely to appear between 10 PM and 4 AM.
- Consider a Guided Tour: Many tour operators offer Northern Lights tours, which can provide valuable insights and increase your chances of spotting the Aurora.

Additional Tips:

- Check the Weather: Cloudy skies can obscure the Aurora. Monitor the weather forecast to plan your viewing accordingly.
- Be Flexible: The Aurora can appear suddenly and disappear quickly. Be flexible and adjust your plans as needed.
- Enjoy the Experience: Even if you don't see the Northern Lights, you can still enjoy the beautiful Icelandic landscape and the tranquility of the night sky.

The Blue Lagoon: A Geothermal Oasis in Iceland

Nestled amidst a lava field on the Reykjanes Peninsula, the Blue Lagoon is a geothermal spa that has become an iconic symbol of Iceland. Renowned for its milky blue waters, soothing mineral properties, and captivating surroundings, the Blue Lagoon offers a unique and rejuvenating experience.

A Geothermal Wonder

The Blue Lagoon's water is heated by geothermal energy, drawing water from deep underground. This water is rich in minerals, including silica, sodium, and sulfur, which are believed to have therapeutic benefits for the skin and hair. The water temperature remains a comfortable 37-40°C (98.6-104°F), making it a perfect place to relax and soak up the warmth.

The Spa Experience

The Blue Lagoon offers a range of spa facilities and treatments to enhance your experience. You can relax in the lagoon's mineral-rich waters, enjoy massages and facials, or try unique in-water treatments like the Silica Mud Mask. The spa also features a sauna, steam rooms, and a cafe where you can enjoy refreshments and snacks.

Beyond the Lagoon

The Blue Lagoon is more than just a spa; it's a unique destination surrounded by stunning natural beauty. You can take a dip in the lagoon and then explore the surrounding lava fields, visit the nearby fishing village of Grindavík, or take a boat tour on the ocean.

Visiting the Blue Lagoon

The Blue Lagoon is open year-round, making it a popular destination for visitors from all over the world. It's recommended to book your tickets in advance, especially during peak season. You can choose from a variety of entrance options, including day visits, comfort packages, and luxury retreats.

Tips for Your Visit:

- Book in advance: Tickets can sell out quickly, especially during peak season.
- Arrive early: Beat the crowds and enjoy some peace and quiet in the morning.
- Bring a swimsuit and towel: The Blue Lagoon provides towels for rent, but you can save money by bringing your own.
- Don't forget sunscreen: Even though the water is warm, the sun can still be strong.
- Relax and enjoy the experience: The Blue Lagoon is a place to unwind and rejuvenate. Take some time to soak in the water and let the stress melt away.

A Must-Visit for Travelers

Whether you're looking for relaxation, rejuvenation, or a unique cultural experience, the Blue Lagoon is a must-visit destination in Iceland. It's a place where you can escape the hustle and bustle of everyday life and connect with nature's healing powers.

Snæfellsnes Peninsula:

Kirkjufellsfoss Waterfall

Kirkjufellsfoss is a small but captivating waterfall located on the Snæfellsnes Peninsula in West Iceland. Its name translates to "Church Mountain Falls," a nod to the distinctive shape of Kirkjufell Mountain that rises majestically behind it.

The Beauty of Kirkjufellsfoss

The waterfall itself is relatively small, cascading down a series of three steps from a height of about 16 meters (52 feet). However, its beauty lies in its setting and unique features. The waterfall is framed by lush green meadows and framed by the majestic Kirkjufell Mountain, creating a picturesque scene that is often featured in postcards and travel brochures.

The water flowing down the waterfall is crystal clear and reflects the surrounding landscape, creating a stunning mirror-like effect. The waterfall is also surrounded by colorful wildflowers, which add to its natural beauty.

Visiting Kirkjufellsfoss

Kirkjufellsfoss is easily accessible by car, and there is a free parking lot near the waterfall. From the parking lot, it is a short walk to the bridge that crosses the river and provides the best views of the waterfall.

There are also several hiking trails in the area, allowing visitors to explore the surrounding landscape and capture stunning photos of the waterfall from different angles.

Kirkjufellsfoss in Popular Culture

Kirkjufellsfoss has become one of the most photographed waterfalls in Iceland, thanks to its stunning beauty and unique charm. It has also been featured in several films and TV shows, including Game of Thrones and The Secret Life of Walter Mitty.

A Must-See for Visitors to Iceland

If you are visiting Iceland, Kirkjufellsfoss is a must-see destination. It is a truly magical place that will leave you awestruck by its natural beauty.

Snæfellsjökull Glacier:

Snæfellsjökull is a glacier located on the Snæfellsnes Peninsula in West Iceland. It is the largest glacier in West Iceland and is home to a variety of wildlife, including Arctic foxes, reindeer, and birds. The glacier is also a popular destination for hiking, skiing, and snowmobiling.

Arnarstapi Village:

Arnarstapi is a small fishing village located on the southern side of the Snæfellsnes Peninsula. It is a popular destination for tourists, and it offers a variety of attractions, including a lighthouse, a museum, and a swimming pool. The village is also home to several restaurants and cafes, as well as a few hotels and guesthouses.

Visiting Snæfellsjökull and Arnarstapi:

There are several ways to visit Snæfellsjökull and Arnarstapi. You can drive to the area from Reykjavik, or you can take a bus or taxi. There are also several tour companies that offer guided tours of the area.

Once you arrive in Arnarstapi, you can walk to the glacier or take a guided tour. There are also several hiking trails in the area, allowing you to explore the surrounding landscape.

Snæfellsjökull and Arnarstapi are two of the most popular attractions on the Snæfellsnes Peninsula. They offer a unique combination of natural beauty, history, and culture.

Other Notable Attractions:

Jökulsárlón Glacier Lagoon: A Glacial Marvel

Jökulsárlón Glacier Lagoon is a stunning natural wonder located in Vatnajökull National Park on Iceland's South Coast. This glacial lagoon is formed by the melting of the Breiðamerkurjökull glacier, one of the largest outlet glaciers of Vatnajökull.

A Glacial Symphony:

The lagoon is a mesmerizing spectacle of icebergs of various sizes, ranging from small chunks to massive blocks that can be as large as houses. These icebergs drift slowly across the lagoon, their colors ranging from deep blue to translucent green. The lagoon is also home to a variety of wildlife, including seals, seabirds, and even the occasional whale.

The Diamond Beach:

The lagoon empties into the Atlantic Ocean, and the icebergs that break away from the lagoon are carried out to sea. Some of these icebergs wash up on the nearby Diamond Beach, where they sparkle like diamonds in the sunlight. This unique beach is a popular destination for photographers and nature lovers.

Visiting Jökulsárlón:

There are several ways to experience Jökulsárlón. Visitors can take a boat tour on the lagoon, which offers a close-up view of the icebergs. You can also hike along the shore and admire the stunning scenery. There are several viewpoints and observation platforms that provide panoramic views of the lagoon and the surrounding area.

Tips for Visiting Jökulsárlón:

- Check the Weather: The weather on the South Coast can be unpredictable. Check the weather forecast before you visit to avoid disappointment.
- Dress Warmly: Even in summer, the weather can be chilly, especially near the lagoon. Dress in warm layers and waterproof clothing.
- Bring a Camera: Jökulsárlón is a photographer's dream. Be sure to bring your camera to capture the stunning scenery.
- Respect the Environment: Jökulsárlón is a fragile ecosystem. Please respect the environment by staying on designated paths and avoiding disturbing wildlife.

Skaftafell National Park: A Land of Ice and Fire

Skaftafell National Park is another must-visit destination on Iceland's South Coast. This park is part of Vatnajökull National Park and offers a diverse range of landscapes, including glaciers, volcanoes, and forests.

Svartifoss Waterfall:

One of the most popular attractions in Skaftafell is Svartifoss, a stunning black waterfall that is surrounded by hexagonal basalt columns. The contrast between the black columns and the white waterfall creates a striking and unique scene.

Hiking Trails:

Skaftafell offers a variety of hiking trails that cater to different fitness levels and interests. You can hike to Svartifoss, explore the Vatnajökull glacier, or take a longer hike to the Morsárjökull glacier.

Glacier Walks:

Guided glacier walks are a popular activity in Skaftafell. These walks offer a unique opportunity to explore the Vatnajökull glacier up close and learn about its geology and history.

Tips for Visiting Skaftafell:

- Check the Weather: The weather in Skaftafell can be unpredictable, especially in winter. Check the weather forecast before you visit.
- Dress Warmly: Even in summer, the weather can be chilly, especially if you're planning to hike on the glacier. Dress in warm layers and waterproof clothing.
- Bring Hiking Boots: The terrain in Skaftafell can be uneven, so it's important to wear comfortable hiking boots.
- Respect the Environment: Skaftafell is a fragile ecosystem. Please respect the environment by staying on designated trails and avoiding disturbing wildlife.

Mývatn Lake Area:

Mývatn Lake is a geothermal lake located in North Iceland. It is surrounded by a number of volcanic craters, lava fields, and hot springs. The lake is home to a variety of birdlife, including swans, geese, and ducks.

Notable Attractions in the Mývatn Lake Area:

- Dimmuborgir: This lava field is a popular destination for hiking and photography. The lava formations create a unique and otherworldly landscape.
- Hverfjall: This volcanic crater is one of the largest in the world. Visitors can hike to the top of the crater and enjoy panoramic views of the surrounding area.
- Námafjall: This geothermal area is home to a number of hot springs and mud pots. The area is also known for its strong sulfur smell.
- Grjótagjá Cave: This cave is a popular spot for swimming, although the water temperature can fluctuate.

Akureyri: Iceland's Northern Capital:

Akureyri is the second-largest city in Iceland and is located in the north of the country. The city is surrounded by mountains and fjords, and it offers a variety of attractions for visitors.

Notable Attractions in Akureyri:

- Akureyri Botanical Garden: This botanical garden is home to a variety of plants from around the world. The garden is also home to a greenhouse and a herb garden.
- Akureyri Art Museum: This museum houses a collection of Icelandic and international art. The museum also hosts temporary exhibitions throughout the year.
- Akureyri Cathedral: This cathedral is the largest church in Iceland outside of Reykjavik. The cathedral is home to a number of stained glass windows and a pipe organ.
- Akureyri Swimming Pool: This swimming pool is a popular destination for locals and tourists alike. The pool features a wave pool, a lazy river, and a hot tub.

Tips for Visiting Mývatn and Akureyri:

- Rent a Car: Renting a car is the best way to get around Mývatn and Akureyri. This will give you the flexibility to explore the area at your own pace.
- Pack Warmly: The weather in North Iceland can be unpredictable, even in summer. Dress in warm layers and waterproof clothing.
- Bring Good Hiking Boots: There are a number of hiking trails in the Mývatn area, so it's important to wear comfortable hiking boots.
- Respect the Environment: Both Mývatn and Akureyri are fragile ecosystems. Please respect the environment by staying on designated paths and avoiding disturbing wildlife.

Winter Activities

Snowmobiling on Vatnajökull Glacier: A Thrilling Adventure

Vatnajökull Glacier, Europe's largest ice cap, offers an unforgettable experience for adventure seekers: snowmobiling. This thrilling activity allows you to explore the vast and icy landscape of the glacier, experiencing its raw beauty and power.

Preparation and Safety:

Before embarking on a snowmobiling adventure, it's essential to prepare and ensure your safety:

- Dress Warmly: Layer up with thermal clothing, waterproof outerwear, and winter boots to protect yourself from the cold and snow.
- Wear a Helmet: A helmet is crucial for your safety while riding a snowmobile.
- Listen to Instructions: Pay close attention to the safety briefing provided by your guide. They will explain the rules of the road and how to operate the snowmobile safely.

- Follow the Guide: Always follow your guide's instructions. They know the terrain and will lead you on safe routes.

The Thrill of Snowmobiling on a Glacier:

Snowmobiling on Vatnajökull Glacier is an exhilarating experience. As you navigate the icy terrain, you'll be surrounded by breathtaking scenery, including towering ice formations, deep crevasses, and stunning vistas.

- Explore the Ice Caves: Many snowmobiling tours include visits to ice caves. These natural wonders are formed by melting water that carves tunnels through the ice. Exploring an ice cave is a truly unique and unforgettable experience.
- Witness the Glacier's Power: The sheer size and power of Vatnajökull Glacier are awe-inspiring. As you ride across its surface, you'll gain a new appreciation for the forces of nature.

- Experience the Thrill of Speed: Snowmobiling is a thrilling activity, and Vatnajökull Glacier provides the perfect playground. Feel the rush of adrenaline as you zip across the icy surface.

Vatnajökull Glacier: A Unique Destination:
Vatnajökull Glacier is a unique destination that offers a variety of activities for visitors. In addition to snowmobiling, you can also go hiking, ice climbing, and glacier walking. The glacier's diverse landscape and stunning scenery make it a must-visit for nature lovers and adventure seekers.

Tips for Snowmobiling on Vatnajökull Glacier:

- Book Your Tour in Advance: Snowmobiling tours can be popular, especially during peak season. Book your tour in advance to secure your spot.

- Choose a Reputable Tour Operator: Select a tour operator with a good reputation and experienced guides.
- Check the Weather: The weather in Iceland can be unpredictable. Check the forecast before your tour to ensure favorable conditions.
- Respect the Environment: Vatnajökull Glacier is a fragile ecosystem. Avoid disturbing the wildlife and stay on designated trails.

Exploring Frozen Caves: A Winter Wonderland Adventure

Ice caves are a mesmerizing natural phenomenon that forms in regions with extreme winter conditions. These subterranean structures offer a unique and enchanting experience for those who dare to venture into their frozen depths.

How Ice Caves Form:

Ice caves typically form in areas with high snowfall and freezing temperatures. Over time, the snow compresses into ice, creating a dense and stable structure. Water seeping through the ice can carve out tunnels and chambers, forming intricate and often otherworldly shapes.

Exploring Ice Caves:

Exploring ice caves requires proper equipment and guidance from experienced professionals.

Here are some key points to remember:

- Safety First: Always prioritize safety when exploring ice caves. Wear appropriate clothing, including warm layers, waterproof gear, and sturdy boots.
- Guided Tours: It's highly recommended to join a guided tour to ensure your safety and gain valuable insights into the formation and history of ice caves.
- Respect the Environment: Ice caves are fragile ecosystems. Avoid touching the walls or disturbing the formations to preserve their beauty for future generations.
- Be Mindful of Falling Ice: Ice caves can be unstable, and there is always a risk of falling ice. Stay alert and follow your guide's instructions.

Famous Ice Caves:

- Vatnajökull National Park, Iceland: This national park is home to numerous ice caves, including the famous Blue Ice Cave. These caves are known for their stunning blue hues and intricate formations.
- Glacier National Park, Montana, USA: Glacier National Park offers opportunities to explore ice caves, particularly in the Logan Pass area. These caves can be accessed through guided tours.
- Skaftafell National Park, Iceland: This national park is another excellent destination for ice cave exploration. The Svartifoss waterfall area is known for its beautiful ice formations.
- Mendenhall Glacier, Alaska, USA: Mendenhall Glacier is home to several ice caves, including the Nugget Ice Cave. These caves are accessible through guided tours and offer a unique experience.

A Winter Wonderland Adventure:

Exploring ice caves is a truly magical experience. The otherworldly beauty of these frozen structures, combined with the thrill of adventure, makes them a must-visit for nature lovers and thrill-seekers alike. Remember to prioritize safety and respect the environment to ensure a memorable and enjoyable experience.

Dog Sledding: A Winter Adventure in Iceland

Dog sledding is a thrilling and unforgettable experience that's particularly popular in Iceland during the winter months. Imagine gliding across a snowy landscape, pulled by a team of energetic and friendly dogs. It's an adventure that combines the beauty of nature with the excitement of winter sports.

A Unique Experience:

Dog sledding offers a unique opportunity to connect with nature and experience the Icelandic winter firsthand. As you ride through the snowy landscapes, you'll be surrounded by breathtaking scenery, including snow-capped mountains, frozen lakes, and icy fjords.

The Dogs:

The dogs used for sledding are typically Siberian Huskies or Alaskan Malamutes. These breeds are known for their endurance, strength, and love of the cold. They are also incredibly friendly and playful, making them ideal for this type of activity.

Guided Tours:

Most dog sledding tours in Iceland are guided, ensuring your safety and providing you with valuable insights into the experience. Your guide will provide you with instructions on how to handle the sled and control the dogs.

Popular Locations:

- Vatnajökull National Park: This national park offers some of the best dog sledding opportunities in Iceland. You can explore the vast glaciers and snow-covered landscapes.
- Snæfellsnes Peninsula: This peninsula offers a more intimate dog sledding experience, with smaller teams of dogs and a more relaxed atmosphere.
- Northern Iceland: The northern regions of Iceland, such as Akureyri and Mývatn, are also popular for dog sledding.

Tips for Dog Sledding:

- Dress Warmly: Layer up with warm clothing, including thermal base layers, a waterproof jacket, and winter boots.
- Wear Gloves: Cold weather can make your hands numb, so it's important to wear gloves or mittens.
- Listen to Your Guide: Follow your guide's instructions carefully to ensure a safe and enjoyable experience.
- Enjoy the Ride: Sit back, relax, and enjoy the thrill of being pulled by a team of energetic dogs.

Northern Lights Tours: Guided Experiences in Iceland

Chasing the Northern Lights, or Aurora Borealis, is a popular activity in Iceland during the winter months. Guided tours offer a convenient and informative way to experience this natural phenomenon. Here's a breakdown of what to expect from a Northern Lights tour:

Tour Highlights:

- Expert Guides: Your guide will have extensive knowledge of the Aurora Borealis and will be able to predict the best viewing conditions and locations.
- Transportation: Most tours include transportation from your accommodation to the viewing spot. This is especially convenient if you're staying in a city or town.
- Warm Clothing and Equipment: Tour operators typically provide warm clothing and equipment, such as thermal suits and snow boots, to keep you comfortable during the cold Icelandic nights.

- Aurora Photography Tips: Your guide will offer tips on how to capture the Northern Lights in stunning photographs.
- Hot Beverages and Snacks: Many tours include hot beverages and snacks to keep you warm and energized.

Choosing a Tour:

When choosing a Northern Lights tour, consider the following factors:

- Duration: Tours can range from a few hours to overnight excursions. Choose a duration that fits your schedule and preferences.
- Group Size: Smaller groups often offer a more personalized experience.
- Price: Prices vary depending on the tour operator, duration, and amenities.
- Location: Some tours focus on specific regions, such as the Golden Circle or the Snæfellsnes Peninsula.

Tips for Northern Lights Tours:

- Check the Aurora Forecast: Before your tour, check the Aurora forecast to get an idea of the viewing conditions.

- Dress Warmly: Even if the forecast predicts clear skies, it's essential to dress warmly. The Icelandic winters can be harsh.

- Be Patient: The Aurora Borealis can be unpredictable. Be patient and enjoy the experience, even if you don't see the lights immediately.

- Follow Your Guide's Instructions: Your guide will have valuable insights and recommendations. Follow their instructions to maximize your chances of seeing the Northern Lights.

- Enjoy the Experience: Northern Lights tours offer a unique opportunity to experience the beauty of Iceland's winter landscape. Relax, enjoy the atmosphere, and hope for a spectacular display of the Aurora.

A guided Northern Lights tour is a great way to experience this natural phenomenon in Iceland. With the help of experienced guides, you can increase your chances of witnessing the Aurora Borealis and capturing stunning photographs. Remember, even if you don't see the lights, the experience of being under the vast Icelandic sky is unforgettable.

Skiing and Snowboarding in Iceland: A Winter Wonderland

While Iceland may not be the first destination that comes to mind for winter sports, it actually offers some excellent opportunities for skiing and snowboarding. With its snow-capped mountains and challenging terrain, Iceland can provide a unique and unforgettable experience for winter sports enthusiasts.

Ski Resorts:

- Hlíðarfjall: Located near Akureyri, Hlíðarfjall is Iceland's largest ski resort. It offers a variety of slopes for skiers and snowboarders of all levels, as well as a terrain park.
- Kerlingarfjöll: This ski resort is located in the central highlands of Iceland and offers stunning views of the surrounding mountains. It has a variety of slopes, including some challenging off-piste terrain.

- Bláfjöll: Located near Reykjavik, Bláfjöll is a popular ski resort for locals and tourists alike. It offers a variety of slopes, as well as a snowpark and a children's area.

Unique Skiing Experiences:
- Glacier Skiing: One of the most unique skiing experiences in Iceland is glacier skiing. This involves skiing on a glacier, which can be challenging but incredibly rewarding.
- Heli-Skiing: For the ultimate adrenaline rush, heli-skiing is available in Iceland. This involves being flown to remote areas of the mountains, where you can ski on untouched powder.

Tips for Skiing and Snowboarding in Iceland:
- Check the Weather: The weather in Iceland can be unpredictable, so it's important to check the forecast before heading out.
- Dress Warmly: Iceland's winters can be cold, so it's important to dress in layers and wear waterproof clothing.

- Rent Equipment: If you don't have your own ski or snowboard equipment, you can rent it at most resorts.
- Take a Lesson: If you're a beginner, it's a good idea to take a lesson to learn the basics.
- Respect the Environment: Iceland's natural environment is fragile. Please respect the environment by staying on designated trails and avoiding disturbing wildlife.

While Iceland may not be as well-known as other winter sports destinations, it offers a unique and unforgettable experience. With its challenging terrain, stunning scenery, and friendly locals, Iceland is a great place to enjoy skiing and snowboarding.

Snowshoeing in Iceland: Exploring the Wilderness

Snowshoeing is a popular winter activity in Iceland, offering a unique way to explore the country's vast and snowy landscapes. With snowshoes, you can traverse terrain that would be inaccessible on foot, allowing you to discover hidden gems and enjoy the peace and tranquility of the Icelandic wilderness.

Popular Snowshoeing Destinations:

- Vatnajökull National Park: This national park offers a variety of snowshoeing trails, ranging from easy to challenging. You can explore glaciers, forests, and volcanic landscapes.
- Langjökull Glacier: This glacier is another popular destination for snowshoeing. You can explore the vast ice fields and even visit ice caves.
- Snæfellsnes Peninsula: This peninsula offers a more intimate snowshoeing experience, with smaller trails and stunning coastal views.

- Landmannalaugar: This geothermal area is a colorful landscape of hot springs, rhyolite mountains, and snow-covered valleys. It's a great place for a snowshoeing adventure.

Tips for Snowshoeing in Iceland:
- Dress Warmly: Layer up with thermal clothing, waterproof outerwear, and winter boots.
- Bring Snowshoes and Poles: These are essential for navigating the snow-covered terrain.
- Follow Trails: Stay on designated trails to avoid getting lost and to protect the environment.
- Respect Wildlife: Be mindful of wildlife and avoid disturbing their habitat.
- Check the Weather: The weather in Iceland can be unpredictable, so check the forecast before heading out.

Benefits of Snowshoeing:

- Exercise: Snowshoeing is a great way to get exercise and burn calories.
- Nature Connection: Exploring the Icelandic wilderness on snowshoes allows you to connect with nature and appreciate its beauty.
- Peace and Quiet: Snowshoeing can be a peaceful and relaxing activity, away from the hustle and bustle of city life.
- Unique Experience: Snowshoeing in Iceland is a unique and unforgettable experience.

Food and Drink

Icelandic Cuisine: A Taste of the North

Icelandic cuisine is a unique blend of traditional Nordic flavors and influences from other cultures. The harsh climate and limited resources of Iceland have shaped its culinary traditions, resulting in dishes that are hearty, flavorful, and often unexpected.

Traditional Icelandic Dishes:

- Fish: As an island nation, Iceland has a rich seafood tradition. Fish is a staple of the Icelandic diet, and it can be prepared in many different ways. Some popular fish dishes include:
  - Hákarl: Fermented shark, a strong-smelling delicacy that is considered a rite of passage for many Icelanders.
  - Graavíða: Smoked fish, often served with rye bread and mustard.
  - Plokkfiskur: Fish stew, made with cod, potatoes, onions, and milk.

- Lamb: Lamb is another popular ingredient in Icelandic cuisine. It is often served as a roast, stew, or kebab.
- Skyr: Skyr is a fermented dairy product that is similar to yogurt but has a thicker texture and a tangier flavor. It is often eaten with berries or honey.
- Rúgbrauð: Icelandic rye bread is a dense and flavorful bread that is often served with smoked fish or lamb.
- Kleina: Kleina are sweet dough balls that are deep-fried and covered in powdered sugar. They are a popular treat in Iceland.
- Laufabrauð: Laufabrauð is a traditional Icelandic flatbread that is made by cutting intricate patterns into the dough before baking. It is often served with smoked lamb or fish.
- Brennivín: Brennivín is a strong Icelandic spirit that is often flavored with caraway seeds. It is traditionally served with hákarl.

Influences on Icelandic Cuisine:

Icelandic cuisine has been influenced by a variety of cultures, including Danish, Norwegian, and British. These influences can be seen in the use of ingredients, cooking methods, and dishes. For example, the Icelandic hot dog is a popular street food that was introduced to Iceland by American soldiers during World War II.

Modern Icelandic Cuisine:

In recent years, Icelandic cuisine has undergone a renaissance. Chefs are experimenting with new ingredients and techniques, creating innovative and delicious dishes. This has led to a growing number of high-quality restaurants in Iceland.

Tips for Trying Icelandic Cuisine:

- Be Adventurous: Icelandic cuisine can be quite different from what you're used to. Don't be afraid to try new things.
- Ask for Recommendations: Locals can often recommend the best places to eat and the most authentic dishes.
- Consider the Seasonality of Ingredients: Some Icelandic ingredients are only available during certain seasons.
- Pair Your Food with Icelandic Beverages: Icelandic beer, wine, and spirits can complement the flavors of Icelandic cuisine.

Local Beverages: A Taste of Iceland

Iceland offers a variety of local beverages that reflect the country's unique culture and history. Here are some of the most popular options:

- Brennivín: This strong Icelandic spirit is often flavored with caraway seeds and is traditionally served with hákarl (fermented shark). It has a strong, pungent taste and is considered an acquired taste by many.

- Bjórbragð: This is a type of Icelandic beer that is made with Icelandic water and barley. It has a slightly sweet and malty flavor.

- Skyr Sykur This is a sweet yogurt drink that is made with skyr (fermented dairy product) and sugar. It is a popular breakfast drink in Iceland.

- Icelandic Coffee: Icelandic coffee is often served in a special mug that keeps it warm for a long time. It is often accompanied by a small donut or a piece of cake.

- Hot Chocolate: Hot chocolate is a popular winter drink in Iceland. It is often served with whipped cream and marshmallows.

Dining Out in Iceland: A Culinary Adventure

Iceland offers a variety of dining options to suit all tastes and budgets. Here are some tips for dining out in Iceland:

- Try Local Cuisine: Icelandic cuisine is unique and delicious. Be sure to try some traditional dishes, such as hákarl, plokkfiskur, and skyr.
- Consider the Seasonality of Ingredients: Some Icelandic ingredients are only available during certain seasons.
- Look for the "Icelandic Label": This label indicates that the restaurant serves authentic Icelandic cuisine.
- Budget for Dining Out: Dining out in Iceland can be expensive, especially in Reykjavik. Be sure to factor dining costs into your budget.

- Consider Food Tours: Food tours are a great way to sample a variety of Icelandic dishes and learn about the country's culinary traditions.

Popular Dining Options:
- Fish Restaurants: Iceland is known for its fresh seafood. There are many excellent fish restaurants throughout the country.
- Reykjavík Restaurants: The capital city offers a wide variety of dining options, from casual cafes to fine dining restaurants.
- Local Food Markets: Visit local food markets to sample a variety of Icelandic products, including cheeses, smoked fish, and jams.
- Street Food: Icelandic street food is becoming increasingly popular. You can find a variety of delicious snacks and meals from street vendors.

Culture and Traditions

Icelandic Sagas and Folklore: A Window into the Past

Icelandic sagas and folklore offer a fascinating glimpse into the country's rich cultural heritage. These stories have been passed down through generations, preserving the traditions and values of the Icelandic people.

Icelandic Sagas:

Icelandic sagas are prose narratives that were written in the 13th century. They are primarily concerned with the history of Iceland's early settlers and their descendants. The sagas are often divided into two categories: family sagas and Icelandic sagas.

- Family Sagas: These sagas focus on the lives of individual families and their relationships with each other. They often involve themes of revenge, honor, and loyalty.
- Icelandic Sagas: These sagas are more concerned with the history of Iceland as a whole. They often involve political intrigue, religious conflict, and the struggle for power.

Famous Sagas:

- Njáls saga: This is one of the most famous Icelandic sagas. It tells the story of Njáll, a wise and peaceful man who is ultimately betrayed by his enemies.
- Egils saga: This saga tells the story of Egil Skallagrimsson, a Viking warrior who becomes a poet and historian.
- Laxdæla saga: This saga tells the story of a powerful family who lives in the Laxárdalur valley. It is a complex story that explores themes of love, betrayal, and revenge.

The Importance of Sagas:

Icelandic sagas are important for several reasons:

- Historical Record: They provide a valuable historical record of Iceland's early history.
- Literary Masterpieces: The sagas are considered to be some of the greatest works of medieval literature.

- Cultural Identity: Sagas have played a significant role in shaping Icelandic culture and identity.

Folklore:

Icelandic folklore is rich and diverse. It includes tales of trolls, elves, and other mythical creatures. Folklore was often used to explain natural phenomena and to teach moral lessons.

Famous Folklore Tales:

- The Hidden People: These are small, mischievous creatures that are said to live in the Icelandic landscape.
- The Troll Church: This is a legend about a group of trolls who were caught in the sunlight and turned to stone.
- The Yule Lads: These are thirteen mischievous boys who visit Icelandic homes during the Christmas season.

The Influence of Folklore:

Icelandic folklore has had a significant influence on Icelandic culture and art. Many Icelandic folk tales have been adapted into films, television shows, and books.

Icelandic sagas and folklore offer a fascinating window into the country's past. These stories have been passed down through generations, preserving the traditions and values of the Icelandic people. By studying Icelandic sagas and folklore, we can gain a deeper understanding of the country's rich cultural heritage.

Icelandic Music and Arts: A Vibrant Scene

Iceland has a thriving music and arts scene that reflects the country's unique culture and history. From traditional folk music to contemporary art, there is something to appeal to everyone.

Icelandic Music:

Icelandic music is characterized by its raw energy, haunting melodies, and innovative approach to songwriting. The country has produced a number of world-renowned musicians, including Björk, Sigur Rós, and Múm.

- Folk Music: Icelandic folk music is rooted in the country's ancient traditions. It often features haunting melodies, complex harmonies, and lyrical storytelling.
- Post-Rock: Iceland has a thriving post-rock scene, with bands like Sigur Rós and Ásgeir leading the way. Post-rock music is characterized by its use of ambient sounds, long instrumental passages, and emotional intensity.

- Experimental Music: Icelandic musicians are known for their experimental approach to music. They often combine traditional elements with electronic sounds and avant-garde techniques.

Icelandic Art:

Icelandic art is diverse and reflects the country's unique landscape and culture. There is a strong tradition of visual arts, including painting, sculpture, and photography.

- Visual Arts: Icelandic artists often draw inspiration from the country's dramatic landscapes and its rich history.
- Literature: Iceland has a strong literary tradition, with authors like Halldór Laxness and Sjón producing acclaimed works of fiction.
- Design: Icelandic design is known for its minimalist aesthetic and use of natural materials.

Festivals and Events:

Iceland hosts a number of festivals and events throughout the year. These events celebrate the country's music, art, culture, and heritage.

- Iceland Airwaves: This annual music festival features a diverse lineup of Icelandic and international bands.
- Reykjavík Art Festival: This festival showcases contemporary art from Iceland and around the world.
- Secret Solstice: This music festival takes place during the summer solstice and features a lineup of international acts.
- Icelandic Design March: This event celebrates Icelandic design and innovation.
- Icelandic Food and Music Festival: This festival showcases Icelandic cuisine and music.

Safety and Etiquette

Safety Tips for Winter Travel

- Dress in warm layers: The weather in Iceland can be unpredictable, even in summer. Dress in warm layers, including base layers, fleece jackets, and waterproof outerwear.
- Bring a winter hat and gloves: Protect your head and hands from the cold with a warm hat and gloves.
- Pack sturdy boots: Good quality waterproof boots are a must-have for exploring Iceland's rugged terrain.
- Check the weather forecast: Before you travel, check the weather forecast to see what to expect. This will help you plan your clothing and activities accordingly.
- Be prepared for icy conditions: Roads can be icy, especially in winter. Drive slowly and carefully, and be aware of black ice.
- Carry an emergency kit: In case of an emergency, it's a good idea to carry a first-aid kit, a flashlight, and some emergency food and water.

- Stay aware of your surroundings: Be aware of your surroundings and stay alert for potential hazards.
- Respect the environment: Iceland is a fragile ecosystem. Please respect the environment by staying on designated trails and avoiding disturbing wildlife.

By following these safety tips, you can help ensure a safe and enjoyable winter trip to Iceland.

Cultural Etiquette

Icelandic culture is very different from the culture of many other countries. It is important to be respectful of Icelandic customs and traditions. Here are some tips for cultural etiquette in Iceland:

- Be polite and respectful: Icelanders are generally friendly and welcoming people. It is important to be polite and respectful when interacting with them.

- Learn a few Icelandic phrases: Learning a few basic Icelandic phrases can show that you're making an effort to understand their culture.
- Respect the environment: Iceland is a beautiful and fragile country. Please respect the environment by staying on designated trails, avoiding littering, and conserving energy.
- Be patient: Icelanders are often slow-paced and relaxed. It is important to be patient and respectful of their pace of life.
- Dress appropriately: Icelanders are generally dressed conservatively. It is important to dress appropriately when visiting public places.

Respecting the Environment

Iceland is a fragile and beautiful country. It is important to respect the environment by following these tips:

- Stay on designated trails: Do not walk off-trail, as this can damage the fragile ecosystem.
- Leave no trace: Pack out all trash and garbage. Do not leave anything behind.
- Respect wildlife: Do not disturb wildlife, and keep a safe distance from them.
- Conserve water: Iceland is a water-scarce country. Be mindful of your water usage and conserve water whenever possible.
- Support sustainable tourism: Choose to support businesses that are committed to sustainability and environmental protection.

Cultural Etiquette

Iceland is a culturally rich country with its own unique customs and traditions. It is important to be respectful of Icelandic culture by following these tips:

- Learn a few Icelandic phrases: This shows that you are making an effort to understand the culture.
- Dress appropriately: Icelanders are generally dressed conservatively. It is important to dress appropriately when visiting public places.
- Be patient: Icelanders are often slow-paced and relaxed. It is important to be patient and respectful of their pace of life.
- Respect personal space: Icelanders generally value their personal space. It is important to give people their space when talking or interacting with them.
- Avoid being loud: Icelanders are generally quiet and reserved. It is important to avoid being loud or disruptive in public places.

Conclusion

Iceland: A Winter Wonderland

Iceland, the Land of Fire and Ice, is a truly magical place to visit, especially during the winter months. The stark contrast between its icy landscapes and geothermal activity creates a unique and unforgettable experience.

A Winter Wonderland:

Iceland transforms into a winter wonderland during the colder months. Snow-capped mountains, frozen waterfalls, and glistening glaciers create a breathtaking backdrop for your adventure. The icy landscapes are perfect for winter activities like snowmobiling, ice caving, and dog sledding.

Chasing the Aurora Borealis:

One of the main attractions of visiting Iceland in winter is the chance to witness the Northern Lights, or Aurora Borealis. These mesmerizing displays of light dance across the night sky, creating a magical and unforgettable experience.

Unique Geothermal Experiences:

Iceland is home to numerous geothermal areas, including the Blue Lagoon, a popular geothermal spa. Relaxing in the warm, mineral-rich waters of the Blue Lagoon is a truly rejuvenating experience.

A Culinary Adventure:

Icelandic cuisine offers a unique blend of flavors and traditions. Enjoy traditional dishes like hákarl (fermented shark), plokkfiskur (fish stew), and skyr (fermented dairy product). Don't forget to try Icelandic hot chocolate and Brennivín, a traditional Icelandic spirit.

Cultural Experiences:

Iceland's rich culture and history are evident throughout the country. Explore historical sites like Thingvellir National Park, visit museums and art galleries, and experience traditional Icelandic music and dance.

Tips for Planning Your Trip:

- Pack Warmly: Iceland's winters can be cold. Pack warm layers, waterproof clothing, and sturdy boots.
- Book Accommodation in Advance: Popular destinations can get booked up quickly, especially during peak season.
- Rent a Car: Renting a car gives you the flexibility to explore Iceland at your own pace.
- Check the Weather Forecast: Iceland's weather can be unpredictable. Check the forecast before planning your activities.
- Respect the Environment: Iceland is a fragile ecosystem. Please respect the environment by staying on designated trails and avoiding disturbing wildlife.

Conclusion:

Iceland is a truly magical destination, especially during the winter months. The stunning landscapes, unique experiences, and friendly people make it a must-visit for anyone seeking a winter wonderland adventure. Whether you're interested in exploring glaciers, chasing the Northern Lights, or simply relaxing in a geothermal spa, Iceland has something to offer everyone.

Planning Your Own Adventure in Iceland

Iceland offers a unique and unforgettable travel experience. Here are some tips to help you plan your own adventure:

1. Determine Your Travel Style:

- Adventure Seeker: If you're looking for an adrenaline-pumping adventure, consider activities like snowmobiling, glacier hiking, and ice caving.
- Nature Lover: Iceland's stunning landscapes offer plenty of opportunities for hiking, photography, and wildlife watching.
- Culture Enthusiast: Explore Iceland's rich history and culture by visiting museums, historical sites, and attending festivals.
- Relaxation Seeker: If you're looking for a peaceful and relaxing getaway, indulge in geothermal spas, soak in hot springs, or simply enjoy the tranquility of the Icelandic countryside.

2. Choose Your Travel Dates:

- Winter (December-March): Experience the magic of the Northern Lights, snow-covered landscapes, and winter activities like snowmobiling and ice caving.
- Spring (April-May): Enjoy milder temperatures, blooming wildflowers, and fewer crowds.
- Summer (June-August): Experience the longest days of the year, ideal for hiking, camping, and outdoor activities.
- Autumn (September-November): Enjoy stunning fall colors, fewer crowds, and comfortable temperatures.

3. Set a Budget:

- Accommodation: Consider hostels, guesthouses, hotels, camping, or farm stays based on your budget and preferences.
- Transportation: Renting a car is convenient, but public transportation and organized tours are also options.

- Activities: Factor in the cost of activities like snowmobiling, glacier hiking, and museum visits.
- Food: Prepare your own meals or dine out at restaurants, depending on your budget.

4. Plan Your Itinerary:

- Research Popular Attractions: Consider visiting the Golden Circle, the Blue Lagoon, Vatnajökull National Park, and Snæfellsnes Peninsula.
- Create a Flexible Itinerary: Allow for spontaneous adventures and unexpected discoveries.
- Consider Day Trips: Explore smaller towns and villages for a more authentic Icelandic experience.

5. Pack Accordingly:

- Warm Clothing: Layer up with thermal clothing, waterproof outerwear, and winter boots, especially if you're visiting during the colder months.

- Comfortable Shoes: Bring sturdy hiking boots or comfortable walking shoes.
- Camera: Capture the stunning Icelandic landscapes and wildlife.
- First-Aid Kit: Pack a first-aid kit for minor injuries.
- International Adapter: If you're using electronic devices, bring an international adapter.

6. Respect the Environment and Culture:

- Leave No Trace: Respect the natural environment by leaving no trace and staying on designated trails.
- Learn a Few Icelandic Phrases: Show respect for the local culture by learning a few basic Icelandic phrases.
- Be Patient: Icelanders are generally laid-back and patient. Respect their pace of life.

Made in United States
Cleveland, OH
07 March 2025

14982392R00068